M000300807

"If you believe that people have no history worth mentioning, it's easy to believe they have no humanity worth defending."
- William Loren Katz

Abandoned History Series

This book is part of the Abandoned History Series published by the Museum of disABILITY History, People Inc., and People Ink Press.

Due to a general reluctance to discuss the way those in need were treated in the past, records and memories of the institutions that served the poor, sick, and disabled are fading into the past — into the world of abandoned history.

The Museum of disABILITY History is committed to preserving the important historical record of these almost-forgotten institutions.

This book is a part of that effort.

Dr. Skinner's Remarkable School
for "Colored Deaf, Dumb, and Blind Children"
1857-1860

James M. Boles, Ed.D. and Michael Boston, Ph.D.

Editor's Note: The exact language of this time has been retained for historical accuracy. No offense is intended toward any individual or group.

Design by Rachel Gottorff, People Inc.

Cover Art by David J. LoTempio, People Inc.
Based on an illustration from the *Mute and the Blind*,
Saturday August 18, 1860: #10, page 80

Publisher: James M. Boles, Ed.D.

ISBN 13: 978-0-9845983-0-4
ISBN 10: 0-9845983-0-8

People Ink Press
in association with the
Museum of disABILITY History
3826 Main Street
Buffalo, New York 14226

PEOPLE INK PRESS
BUFFALO

Acknowledgements

Many dedicated historians, archivists, librarians, and historical societies provided invaluable resources in putting together the story of Dr. Platt H. Skinner and his remarkable school. The authors relied particularly on the people and resources of the Niagara County Historical Society, Buffalo and Erie County Historical Society, Gallaudet University, Oberlin College, Niagara Falls Public Library, and Old Sturbridge Village. This publication was created through the efforts of many individuals, including Melissa Royer, Michelle Green, Reid Dunlavey, Brian Pietrus, David LoTempio, Sallie Randolph, Rachel Gottorff, Sandra Cassidy, and Tracy Harrienger, along with the capable staff and interns of the Museum of disABILITY History and People Inc. Thank you.

Dedicated to a pioneer in the helping services,
Dr. William J. Woolbright
Huntington Beach, California

James M. Boles, Ed.D.

To the abolitionists who struggled to end slavery.

Michael Boston, Ph.D.

Van Aken ✠ ELMIRA, N.Y.

PLATT HENRY SKINNER
Photo courtesy Gallaudet University

A note to the reader: In order to preserve historical accuracy and to capture a sense of the times, this book quotes some of the exact language from the period when Dr. Skinner ran his school. Please be assured that no offense is intended toward any individual or group.

A controversial pioneer of education, Dr. Platt H. Skinner, ran a remarkable school for African-American children who were blind, deaf, or both. The School for the Instruction of Colored Deaf, Dumb and Blind Children was located in the hamlet of Suspension Bridge, New York, now known as Niagara Falls, New York.

In 1858, Dr. Skinner, a deeply religious white man with progressive blindness, and his young wife, who was hearing impaired, arrived in Suspension Bridge. They were seeking a location where he would establish his second boarding school for African–American children who were disabled.

The Skinners had journeyed north to Niagara after a devastating fire at his first school in Washington, D.C. In Washington, Dr. Skinner had been accused of neglect and was forced to leave his school. Because he was an outspoken abolitionist and believed in racial equality, one could assume the charges

> *The Skinners had journeyed north to Niagara after he was forced to leave his first school.*

against him may not be accurate. The students from Dr. Skinner's Washington school would become the nucleus of a famous institution for the education of the deaf, Gallaudet University.

Dr. Skinner was educated at Oberlin College in Ohio. According to Oberlin College records, he was enrolled in the Preparatory Department from 1843 to 1846. He then trained as a dentist and practiced dentistry in New York City from 1851 to 1855. In 1854 the New York Times carried an announcement that Platt H. Skinner and Jerusha M. Mills had been married by the Rev. Thomas Gallaudet.

From all accounts, Dr. Skinner's school was a happy and productive place. Students learned to communicate through sign language. They were encouraged to help each other and to complement each other's abilities. "We must teach the hand of the mute to perform the office of the tongue, and the eye to perform the office of the ear; the fingers of the blind must be taught to

The Gallaudet Connection

The Gallaudet family was prominent in the history of education of the deaf. Its patriarch, Thomas Hopkins Gallaudet (1787-1851), started the first school for deaf education in Hartford, Connecticut. This school later became the American School for the Deaf.

The elder son, Rev. Thomas Gallaudet (1822-1902), was an Episcopal priest. He worked among the deaf and founded St. Ann's Church for Deaf Mutes in New York City. It is a sign of the regard in which Dr. Skinner was held by the Gallaudet family that Rev. Gallaudet performed the marriage ceremony of Platt and Jerusha Skinner.

The younger son, Edward Miner Gallaudet (1837-1917), became the first superintendent of the first college for the deaf in 1864. Some of the students from Dr. Skinner's first school were part of that college, which eventually became Gallaudet University in Washington, D.C.

A train crosses toward Canada on the upper level of the famous suspension bridge. Foot and horse traffic crossed on the lower level. The suspension bridge was touted as the only railway route to Canada.

> *From all accounts, Dr. Skinner's school was a happy and productive place.*

see," Dr. Skinner wrote in an 1858 report (reproduced in its entirety at the end of this publication).

A visitor to the school, Mrs. Julia Watson, provides an early description: "At the suspension bridge we found an Asylum for the deaf, dumb, and blind. It was a private school kept by Dr. Skinner and his wife. The Doctor had been blind two years – his wife, though she could see, was a mute. This worthy couple, though white themselves, were deeply interested in the poor colored children afflicted like themselves, and their pupils are all colored. Those who could see had bright sparkling eyes, were quiet and respectful. The blind were very tidy and attentive. They

This is a view of the lower roadway of the suspension bridge from the American side facing Canada. The large sign above the two men sitting on the right indicates there was a concern that people marching across might cause the bridge to sway. This concern was so great that the fine was a small fortune in those days: "A fine of $50 to $100 will be imposed for marching over the bridge…"

Dr. Skinner published a newspaper, *The Mute and the Blind*, from 1859 through the mid-1860s. Copies of some issues are available for research at a number of libraries and archives. See the bibliography on page 37 for more information.

Page No. 24

SCHEDULE 1.—Free Inhabitants in _____ of Niagara _____ in the County of Niagara _____ State of New York _____ enumerated by me, on the _____ 11th _____ day of July, 1860. _____

Post Office Niagara Falls _____

The name of every person whose usual place of abode on the first day of June, 1860, was in this family.	Age.	Sex.	Color, { White, black, or mulatto.	Profession, Occupation, or Trade of each person, male and female, over 15 years of age.	Place of Birth, Naming the State, Territory, or Country.	Married within the year.	Attended School within the year.	Persons over 20 y'rs of age who cannot read & write.	Whether deaf and dumb, blind, insane, idiotic, pauper, or convict.	
2	4	5	6	7	10	11	12	13	14	
Dott M. Skinner	30	M		Teacher of deaf & dumb	N. Y.				Blind	15
Amisha	29	F			N. Y.					16
Henry	4	M			N. Y.					17
Betsy Smith	17	F		Bachelor of Divinity Poor Jersey	Canada				Blind	18
James	18	M			Canada					19
Emma Morrison	14	F		Student	Penn.				Blind	20
Nancy Smith	10	F		Student	Canada				Blind	21
Jane Sly	14	F								22
Samuel Sears	11	M		Student						23
Joab	16	M								24
Christian Richards	13	M			Ireland					25
Amanda Robb	14	F								26
Eliza Wilson	8	F			N. Y.					27
Emily Bacon	10	M		Printer	Ireland					28

177

This page from the record of the United States Census of 1860 lists the residents of Dr. Skinner's school. At that time Dr. Skinner was listed as a 30 year-old blind male. Other residents listed included his wife, four year-old son, students and a printer.

> *The paper was sold in the local community and sent to supporters of the school by mail. It was also used as a vehicle for raising funds and as a training tool for the students.*

all seemed very contented and happy, and it was interesting to see the dumb scholars converse with their blind associates.

"The institution is supported partly by donations and contributions from those who sympathize in the good work, and partly by the publication of the paper – the work is done by the pupils who are printers and compositors.

"We came away much pleased with our visit and praying for the success and prosperity of the Asylum, and for the welfare of the generous instructors and founders." (From *Before They Could Vote*, page 215. See the bibliography on page 37.)

In addition to running the school, Dr. Skinner published a

Dr. Skinner's Newspaper

"Then shall the eyes of the blind be opened and the ears of the deaf shall be unstopped."

With this quote, Dr. Platt H. Skinner introduced readers to the semi-monthly newspaper he distributed widely to supporters and throughout the community. Topics ranged from a lengthy description of what had happened at the burned and closed Washington school, to quotes from the Bible, and admonitions from preachers. Many of the articles addressed slavery and education for "Blacks," especially for those who were blind, deaf, or both. The exact dates of publication are unknown but are thought to be from 1859 to the mid-1860s. We have reproduced "clippings" from *The Mute and the Blind* throughout this publication.

THE COLORED PEOPLE OF CANADA—The fugitive slaves in Canada, most of whom, in spite of the diatribes of the New York Herald and papers of that ilk, are living comfortably, propose to found, for the relief and sustenance of new comers among them, an "Agricultural, Mechanical and Education Association," the object of which shall be to give temporary employment and some rudiments of education to emigrants from the Southern States, who, for the most part, arrive among them utterly destitute.

The colored citizens of Toronto have recommended the colored people of Canada to meet in convention on the first day of August next, in the city of Toronto, for the purpose of collecting a full set of statistics of the state and condition of their people, and to discuss any subject which may be calculated to promote their condition.

Excerpt from *The Mute and the Blind.*

newspaper, *The Mute and the Blind.* The paper was sold in the local community and sent to supporters of the school by mail. It was also used as a vehicle for raising funds and as a training tool for the students. "We find by experience that, a blind boy can run our press with about as much speed, as a man who has his sight, and can perform equally as good labor," Dr. Skinner wrote in one article. "Thus, our press is now run: A blind boy at the helm; a deaf-mute girl to arrange the sheets, and a deaf-mute roller."

Finding the funds to keep the school going was a constant struggle for Dr. Skinner and his wife. His various writings in the newspaper and reports are filled with appeals for financial support. The school had nine students in 1858 and Dr. Skinner hoped to increase the number to twenty by the next year, but only if the means could be found. "We are engaged in teaching a class of the most despised and unfortunate creatures in the world. We need help to carry on this work," he wrote in one issue of his

> *The school's location was probably not a coincidence, given Dr. Skinner's passionate abolitionist views. The bridge offered an easy passage to Canada and freedom for fugitive slaves.*

newspaper. "My brother, shall these poor children be shut out from the sympathies of your heart," he implored in the flowery language typical of those times. "I trust not."

The school's location was probably not a coincidence, given Dr. Skinner's passionate abolitionist views. The bridge offered an easy passage to Canada and freedom for fugitive slaves. Both the top train and track and the lower roadway were used in the Underground Railroad. The lower deck was opened in 1854, with Canada only 825 feet away. The proximity of the bridge, in fact, may have been a primary factor in the selection of the Niagara site.

This newspaper drawing of the suspension bridge shows the United States on the left, Canada on the right, and the Niagara River flowing through the deep gorge below.

Fugitive Slave Communities in Canada

The suspension bridge connected New York with Canada and the terminus of the Underground Railroad. Dr. Skinner was known to have relationships with the Canadian fugitive slave communities. Many of the children at his school were sons and daughters of former slaves living in Canada. The border between the United States and Canada became more important after Congress passed the Fugitive Slave Act of 1850. That controversial law required states to arrest and return runaway slaves, so for many, Canada was the only option for freedom.

Dr. Skinner discussed the location of the school in an 1858 report, reproduced in its entirety at the end of this publication. "The question of locality is one of vital importance to such a school. On the one hand, we have pupils from Canada, whose friends are exceedingly tenacious about their children going far toward the borders of what seems to them a most horrid pit-hole – I mean the borders of slavery. On the other hand, we have pupils from the southern States,

> Now, what shall we do, shall we give it up? Shall we say as American citizens that we cannot educate these children because they are black? We have openly declared as a people that we can and will educate the mute and the blind children of the white man. Now on the other hand shall we give it up and admit that we cannot, we will not educate the mute and the blind children of the black man.

Excerpt from *The Mute and the Blind*.

whose friends complain that it is too far north where we now are; they urge that their children cannot endure the extreme cold of the

The Underground Railroad
Slaves and the people who helped them to escape used Railroad terms to code their activities:

LINE....................a route from safe house to
safe house.

STATION...............a safe house where fleeing slaves
could hide.

STOCKHOLDERS.....providers of food and clothing for
fugitive slaves.

CONDUCTORS........people who helped transport
slaves from station to station.

One of the more well-known conductors on the Underground Railroad was Harriet Tubman who led many escapees across the suspension bridge to safety on the other side of the Niagara River in Canada. By 1858, when Dr. Skinner located his school in Suspension Bridge, there were several established communities of fugitive slaves established nearby in Canada. Historians are unsure, but there is reason to believe that Dr. Skinner himself was a conductor on the Underground Railroad.

> *Many fugitive slaves passed through Niagara and over the suspension bridge to Canada on the 'Underground Railroad.'*

climate. Such an institution should be located so as to accommodate the largest number of those who are likely to need its benefits. Such a question as this cannot be decided in a day."

Suspension Bridge was not thickly settled in the 1850s and there were only a few buildings along this section of the Lewiston Road (now Main Street in Niagara Falls) where

"Then Shall the Eyes of the Blind be Opened, and the Ears of the Deaf Shall be Unstopped."

VOL. II.   NIAGARA CITY, SATURDAY, APRIL. 21, 1860.   NO. 3.

THE MUTE AND THE BLIND,

IS PUBLISHED SEMI-MONTHLY AT
NIAGARA CITY, N. Y.

TERMS OF SUBSCRIPTION:
Single copy, ... $1 00
Ten copies to 1 Address, ... 5 00
and at the same rate for any additional number.
All payments strictly IN ADVANCE.
Any person sending two new subscribers will be entitled to this paper for one year.
All communications for THE MUTE AND THE BLIND should be addressed to
P. H. SKINNER,
NIAGARA CITY, N. Y.

EXCITING NEWS FROM MASSACHUSETTS

THE HARPER'S FERRY AFFAIR.

Arrest of Frank B. Sanborn One of the Witnesses—Summoned by the Senate Committee—Rescue—Public Excitement ---His Discharge.

BOSTON Wednesday April 4.

F. B. Sanborn was arrested at Concord, by United States officers last night, under a requisition from the Senate Committee. Watson Freeman, Jr., Deputy United States Marshal, and Silas Carleton, Deputy Sergeant-at-Arms of the United States Senate, called at Sanborn's residence at nine o'clock last night. Sanborn refused to accompany them, when he was handcuffed and taken to a carriage at the door, during which he struggled violently, and the members of his family cried murder, fire, &c. The excitement spread and the bells were rung, collecting a large crowd. Rufus Hosmer, a citizen, died suddenly, it is supposed from the excitement the affair occasioned him. Sanborn was forcibly taken from the officers by the crowd and kept out of their power until a writ of habeas corpus could be obtained. Judge Hoar of the Supreme Court having been applied to, issued a writ of habeas corpus. Deputy-Sheriff John B. Moore served the writ and arrested Sanborn, which ended the Mission of the United States Marshal's posse for the time being. The supreme Court of Massachusetts have decided the proceeding to be illegal and have liberated Mr Sanborn

STATEMENT OF MR. SANBORN.

The following address to the people of Massachusetts appears in the Boston Journal of last evening.

CONCORD, Mass., April 3, 1860. }
12 o'clock at night   }

To the Citizens of 'Massachusetts:

I have to inform you that a cowardly assault was committed on me this evening, at about nine o'clock, *in my own house,* by four or five persons claiming to have authority to arrest me. The facts are these:

I came in from a call about 9 o'clock, and was sitting in my slippers at my desk, when a knocking called me to the door. I went down stairs, opened the door, when a small man entered, and said, "Does Mr. Sanborn live here?" "That is my name, sir," said I, putting out my hand to welcome him. "Here is folded one, which I took.

At that moment, a gray-haired, tall, and stout man, entered the open door, and said, "I arrest you Mr. Sanborn." "By what authority," said I, "and what is your name?" He gave no name, but said, "I am from the United States Marshal's office," or something of that sort. "What is your authority—your warrant," repeated I. "We have a warrant," said some one, for by this time two more men appeared. "Show it—read it," said I. A small man calling himself Freeman, (afterwards, for none would give their names,) began to read a paper, but had only got through a few lines, when the gray-haired ruffian took a pair of handcuffs from his pocket, and proceeded to put them on my wrists, I standing in my own house, without a hat or boots, only in slippers of cloth.

A whistle was given; some men rushed in, none of them known to me, and carried me by force to the street, where stood a carriage with two horses. They lifted me from the ground and tried to put me in the carriage. I resisted with my feet, for my hands were fast in the manacles. They tried two or three times without success, breaking the carriage, but the horses started, and they could not get me in. In the meantime, my cries, and those of my sister, had called my neighbors from their homes, who surrounded the ruffians, and prevented them from carrying me off.

I stood in the street, in my slippers, half an hour, wearing the handcuffs, until Deputy-Sheriff Moore, took me by force from the ruffians' hands, under a writ of habeas corpus issued by Judge Hoar. Their names, given after a long time, and

reluctantly, were Silas Carlton, ——Coolidge, ——Tarleton and Freeman. There were two or three others whose names I have not learned.

Fifteen minutes after I was handcuffed standing in the street, Freeman read me a warrant, signed by Vice President Breckenridge, for my arrest, with an indorsement from McNair, Sergeant-at-arms of U. S. Senate, authorizing Silas Carleton to seize me. How he did it I have said. People of Massachusetts, act as it seems to you best in this case.

F. B. SANBORN.

A little deaf and dumb boy at an examination at the Institution in London, a few years ago, on being asked "Who" "In the beginning God created the heavens and earth."

A clergyman then inquired in a similar manner, "Why did Jesus come into the world?" when again the little boy, with a bright smile on his countenance, indicating delight and gratitude, wrote:

"This is a faithful saying, and worthy of all acceptation that Jesus Christ came into the world to save sinners."

A third question was then proposed evidently adapted to call the most powerful feelings into exercise.

"Why were you born deaf and dumb, while I can hear and speak!"

"Never," said an eye witness, "shall I forget the resignation which sat upon his countenance, as he took the chalk and wrote, 'Even so Father, for so it seemed good in Thy sight,'"

THREE FOUNTAINS.—The fountain of cold water—springs up from the earth,—The fountain of life—opened by the savior of mankind. The fountain of intoxicating drink—gushing from rum shops. To drink at the first of these fountains is to secure health. To drink at the second procures eternal life. To drink at the last named, is to destroy the health of the body and of the mind—the life that now is and that which is to come. *Boys! BOYS!! BOYS!!!* stay away from the last named fountain!
J. S. H.

The run of sap this year is remarkable, and the maple sugar crop of Vermont, this season is estimated at 12,000 to 15,000 tons.

The Mute and the Blind ran eight to ten broadsheet pages (about 11 by 17 inches). A single copy sold for a dollar. Ten copies were five dollars.

> *You're a free man, Joe!*
> *Come and look at the Falls!*

THE MUTE AND THE BLIND

SATURDAY, NOV. 3, 1860

HOW THIS PAPER IS PUBLISHED

The Editor is a blind man; the compositors are deaf and dumb; the press-work is performed by the blind; the papers are folded by the blind and wrapped by mutes.

NOTICE

Our Post Office address will hereafter be Niagara Falls. All communications either for the School or the Mute and the Blind should be directed to P.H. Skinner, Niagara Falls, NY.

Excerpt from *The Mute and the Blind*.

Dr. Skinner's school was located. Many fugitive slaves passed through Niagara and over the suspension bridge to Canada on the "Underground Railroad." Many an abolitionist rode the train over that bridge together with a cargo of fugitive slaves, leading them to freedom.

Harriet Tubman, a famous African-American former slave who led many slaves to freedom as a "Conductor" on the Underground Railroad, once accompanied Joe, a fugitive slave, on a train across the suspension bridge. Upon reaching the Canadian side, she is said to have rushed across the aisle, shaken Joe and shouted, "You've shook de lion's paw, Joe! You're a free man, Joe! Come and look at the Falls!" Joe, it is said, broke down in tears and praised and thanked God.

During the times shortly before the Civil War, Suspension Bridge

---

REPORT OF THE COMMITTEE OF EXAMINATION

We, the undersigned having attended the Examination of the Deaf and Dumb and Blind colored children under the Tuition of Dr. P. H. Skinner in the Village of Niagara City, N.Y. have great pleasure in attesting to the general proficiency of the pupils. The Blind children read with considerable ease from the Raised Lettered Volumes issued by the Bible Society; their acquaintance with English Grammar was tested and their progress was pleasing; in the Sign-Language the Deaf and Dumb answered with ease and grace, and committed to writing on the Black Board appropriate replies to every question proposed.

The children are acquiring the art of Printing; they can set up the types and perform all the other operations essential to the trade of Printing with remarkable facility and accuracy. They are also acquiring the Elements of Arithmetic; and their knowledge of Divine Truth must gratify every benevolent mind.

We recommend cordially Dr. Skinner and his Institution to the sympathy and benevolence of the public assured that in contributing to aid this enterprise they will appropriate their money to a most deserving object and help to sustain and cheer an unjustly vituperated man.

Excerpt from *The Mute and the Blind.*

and other villages and cities in Niagara County were rife with abolitionist and states' rights factions. The *Niagara City Herald,* a local newspaper, supported the states' rights position. States' rights proponents claimed that it was for the state to decide whether or not to permit slavery. In Lockport, the county seat, frequent conflicts occurred between the abolitionists and the supporters of slavery.

14

The buildings above are located on the site of the school today at 1810 Main Street (formerly Lewiston Avenue) in Niagara Falls. In 1858 the school was located above a grocery store at 26 Lewiston Avenue, Suspension Bridge. The center building above is roughly at the same location as Dr. Skinner's school.

By the mid-1800s, Niagara Falls had become a major tourist attraction. Many local business owners and residents were involved in the tourist industry. They were mindful that wealthy plantation owners frequented the Niagara Falls area, sometimes accompanied by slaves. Local owners of shops and other establishments were reluctant to offend such tourists. Community leaders were undoubtedly aware that they could lose business if the abolitionists were permitted to stir things up. Dr. Skinner, as an abolitionist and activist who boldly let his views be known, orally and in print, was regarded as a threat by the pro-slavery faction.

Being a promoter of equality for all racial groups, Dr. Skinner

> *Being a promoter of equality for all racial groups, Dr. Skinner supported the anti-slavery activities of others and may have even been a conductor on the Underground Railroad.*

supported the anti-slavery activities of others and may have even been a conductor on the Underground Railroad. Dr. Skinner interacted regularly with the Canadian fugitive slave communities and reported on them in his newspaper. Many of the children at his school were sons and daughters

> *Dr. Skinner's intense personality, his fierce views, his ardent support of abolition, his newspaper, and his remarkable school combined to make him a controversial figure. During a volatile time in United States history he made many loyal friends, but just as many angry enemies.*

of former slaves living in Canada. The border between the United States and Canada had become vitally important after Congress passed the Fugitive Slave Act of 1850. That controversial law required states to arrest and return fugitive slaves, so for many, Canada was the only option for freedom.

Dr. Skinner's intense personality, his fierce views, his ardent support of abolition, his newspaper, and his remarkable school combined to make him a controversial figure. During a volatile time in United States history he made many loyal friends, but just as many angry enemies. During the time immediately preceding the Civil War, Dr. Skinner and his school became a victim of growing public pressure in Niagara Falls. When the pressure became too intense, he and his wife moved the school to its third and final location in Trenton, New Jersey. Dr. Skinner died in 1866. Shortly after his death, the Trenton School also was burned.

Jan 1. - SKINNER, Dr. P.H., a blind man, editor of the magazine, *The Mute and the Blind* and the first instructor in this country of colored, blind and deaf mute children, for whose sakes he sacrificed all his property, died at Trenton, N.J.

Dr. Skinner's death on January 1, 1866 was among the deaths of prominent individuals reported in the *Necrology of 1866* published by the *New York Times* at the beginning 1867. Each year in January the *Times* published a listing of deaths that had taken place during the previous year.

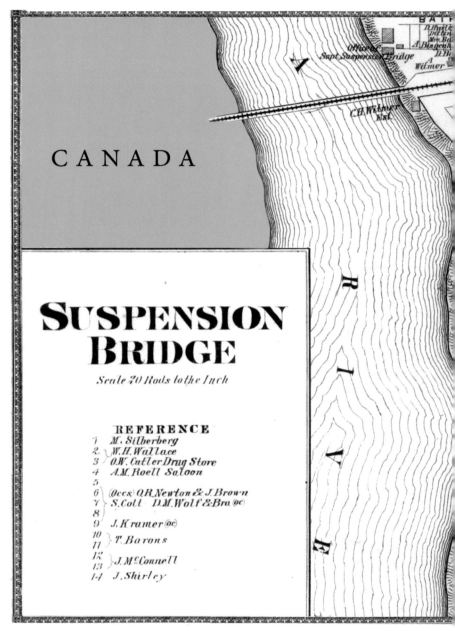

The highlighted block on this 1875 map indicates the approximate location of the school at 26 Lewiston Road as it would have been in 1858. Suspension Bridge is now part of modern Niagara Falls, New York.

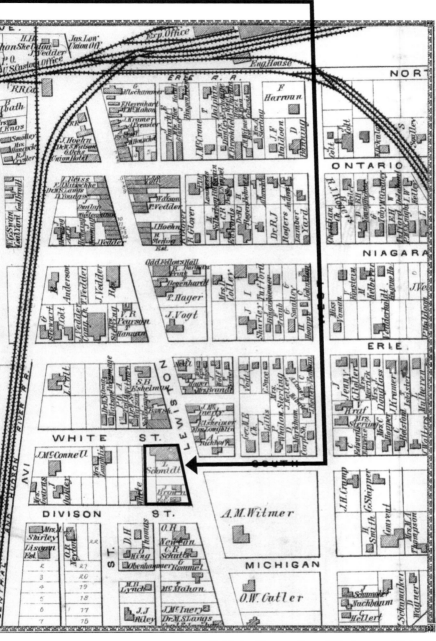

Published in an atlas of Niagara and Orleans Counties in 1875 by D.G. Beers & Company.

The First Semi-Annual Report of the School for the Instruction of the Colored Deaf, Dumb and Blind

This report, reproduced on the following pages in its entirety, provides invaluable insight into the pioneering educational efforts of Dr. Platt H. Skinner. It was apparently produced as a reaction to complaints that Dr. Skinner did not keep detailed-enough records and adequately acknowledge donors to the school.

The publication provides many fascinating hints at the day to day operations of the school and Dr. Skinner's efforts to keep it going. It lists 287 donors and itemizes the donations from dollar amounts right down to the number of eggs provided. The names of many early Western New York families and institutions appear in the report. On page nine, Dr. Skinner hints at the school's eventual relocation to New Jersey in 1860.

This report is a poignant look at the enormous challenges faced by Dr. Skinner and his wife as they struggled during tumultuous times to provide for and educate their deaf and blind African-American students.

THE FIRST SEMI-ANNUAL REPORT

OF THE

School for the Instruction

OF THE

COLORED DEAF, DUMB, AND BLIND

LOCATED AT

NIAGARA CITY, SUSPENSION BRIDGE, N.Y.

P. H. SKINNER, PRINCIPAL.

BUFFALO:
COMMERCIAL ADVERTISER STEAM PRESS.

1858.

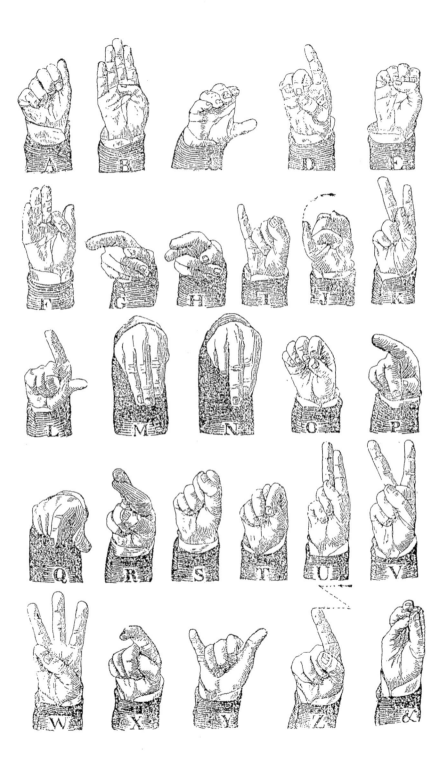

Report of Committee of Examination.

NIAGARA CITY, July 30th, 1858.

The undersigned, having been requested by DR. SKINNER to act as a Committee of Examination for the SCHOOL FOR COLORED DEAF AND DUMB AND BLIND CHILDREN under his charge, take pleasure in stating that the progress of the pupils has, in our view, been rapid and remarkable, and highly creditable to the teachers. Their improvement in manners and general appearance, also, has been very great and commendable. They seem to be neat, contented, cheerful, and happy.

J. O. KNAPP,
Pastor Cong'l Church, Niag. City.

A. McCALL,
Pastor Presbyterian Church, Niag. Falls.

JOS. L. BENNETT,
Pastor Cong'l Church, Lockport.

FIRST SEMI-ANNUAL REPORT

OF THE

School for the Instruction

OF THE

COLORED DEAF, DUMB AND BLIND.

This school was commenced on the first of January, 1858, for the purpose of ameliorating the condition of one of the most unfortunate class of children the world contains. It is not intended to take any child whose education is provided for in any other way. The school was at first established for the children of fugitives; but, since its commencement, it has been thought best to open its doors to all such mute and blind colored children as are not provided for otherwise, as far as the means of the school will permit. The command given us is, " Go into all the world, and preach the gospel to every creature."—This command seems to reach the lowest of all God's creation.

The credentials which are necessary for admission into this school, then, are,

1st. A dark face.

2d. Deaf ears and a mute tongue, or blind eyes.

3d. That the State or country in which they live has not provided for their education.

Then it is intended to take none but those who are in heathenish darkness, and who, without this school, are without the knowledge of a God — no Christ! no heaven! no eternal joys for them! children of the despised race! We find them scattered here and there, fit subjects of mercy. It is believed that the same philanthropy, the same christianity, not to say humanity, that leads to the education of all others, will also provide for these, if we shall succeed in presenting their claims to the public. We believe that

God wants them in Heaven, that angels will welcome them there, and that Christ will crown them with eternal bliss. But it is necessary, before we can preach the gospel to them, that we give them a language by which we may communicate to them their relations to God and the universe. We must teach the hand of the mute to perform the office of the tongue, and the eye to perform the office of the ear; the fingers of the blind must be taught to see. This is our first great field of labor, and it is this that requires toil and expense. This we must do before we can tell them there is a God. It is intended, in this school, to prepare them for usefulness in the world, and enable them to do much toward providing for themselves. Each will be taught to do what he can.

The highest number of pupils in the school during the past term has been nine. It is now ascertained that there are upwards of fifty such children that could be brought into school, if the funds were provided to defray the expenses. It is our wish and intention to increase the number to twenty on the next term, if the means of support can be obtained. The object is a new one; few had ever thought there were such children who needed our aid.

They are scattered in almost every direction. To seek out these little children, and bring them together into a school for the first time, has been no small task. To provide for their continual wants is our next labor. In order to do this, it is necessary to make known their condition to those who have hearts to feel for the unfortunate in their need. We have been called upon to plead the cause of those whose silent tongues cannot speak for themselves; to make the wants of these children known, has been no small part of our labor. During the first six months, from the first of January to the first of July, we have spoken in various places, and under different circumstances, one hundred and thirty-four times, in churches, seminaries, academies, colleges, universities, Sabbath schools, on steamboats and rail-cars—we have ceased not to plead their cause, day nor night.

Rightly to appreciate the trials connected with the labors of this school, we must leave our peaceful home, with all its sunshine and joys, and go to some distant, strange village, rent a tenement sufficient to contain yourself and a few children; now commence your search for the most unfortunate, despised, untutored, uncared for, in many cases the most filthy, and in some cases the most stupid creatures the world ever produced. Now, take off their rags, and replace them with clean and comfortable garments, and keep them replaced day by day. They have no language by which you may communicate with them, or they with themselves. You have now your task before you. Shut yourself up with them one month, and try it, and then tell me if you would not be willing to give a few dollars to aid in such a work, rather than spend the next month in such a way.

All this labor has fallen upon my wife and myself; and this, too, almost entirely without compensation. To commence, carry forward, and establish upon a permanent basis such an institution, is indeed a great work, one requiring endurance. It is our earnest desire to place this school on a firm basis. We hope to be able to announce, in our next semi-annual report, a complete organization.

It is our plan to have a certain number of life-members formed, by the contribution of ten dollars each. It will then be the privilege of these life-members to vote in the trustees and officers of the Institution. Already a part of the contemplated number of life-members has been made up.

The question of locality is one of vital importance to such a school. On the one hand, we have pupils from Canada, whose friends are exceedingly tenacious about their children going far toward the borders of what seems to them a most horrid pit-hole — I mean toward the borders of slavery. On the other hand, we have pupils from the southern States, whose friends complain that it is too far north where we now are; they urge that their children cannot endure the extreme cold of the climate. Such an institution should be located so as to accommodate the largest number of those who are likely to need its benefits. Such a question as this cannot be decided in a day.

We desire to render our sincere thanks to all those who have contributed in any way to aid in ameliorating the condition of the little ones under our care. We hope and pray for the continual guidance of Him who loves these poor unfortunate little ones infinitely more than any man; and with His blessing, we hope to see our efforts crowned with full success.

The great question now being solved is, Shall the unfortunate deaf and dumb or blind colored children be educated, or
not? May we not expect an answer from some friends of the
unfortunate? Shall we increase our number, or not?

Acknowledgments of Donations.

CASH.

Rev. J. L. Bennet, Lockport,	$2 00	
Judge Hiram Gardner, do.	2 00	
Rev. B. D. Marshall, do.	1 00	
Pres. S. S. by A. Scovill, do.	2 50	
Baptist S. S. do.	5 83	
Congregational S. S. do.	3 00	
Union School, do.	8 35	
M. A. Root, Luthr'n S. S. do.	1 90	
Mrs. Helen Holmes, do.	30	
A. Charlton, do.	1 00	
Rev. A. Mc Coll, Niagara Falls, N. Y.	2 00	
Miss Lavinia Porter, do.	25 00	
P. B. Porter, do.	10 00	
Samuel D. Porter, Rochester, N. Y.	1 00	
Mrs. S. B. Stocking, Buffalo,	5 00	
Mrs. A. M. Fish, do.	25	
S. G. Austin, do.	2 00	
Public School, do.	60	
Geo. Gildersleeve, do.	1 00	
Rev. G. W. Heacock, do.	2 00	
Mrs. Shepherd, do.	1 00	
Mrs. S. H. Seymour, do.	1 00	
S. A. Provost, do.	25	
Mrs. Heacock, do.	3 00	
Mr. Ketchum, do.	1 00	
Mrs. Riley, do.	5 00	
J. P. Rich, do.	2 00	
A. Rich, do.	25	
Mrs. J. M. Ganson, do.	2 00	

Mrs. Dr. Burwell, Buffalo.	1 00	
Mrs. Sears, do.	25	
T. A. Hopkins, do.	1 00	
Mrs. Clark, do.	88	
Mrs. Henry Sage, do.	1 00	
Mrs. Geo. Davis, do.	1 00	
Mrs. Sturges, do.	25	
Colored Methodist Church, London, C. W.	1 25	
Received at Lecture, Chatham, C. W.	4 00	
Presbyterian Church, Albion N. Y.	2 00	
Young Ladies Seminary, do.	14 00	
Received by Rev. J. O. Fillmore, Batavia, N. Y.	8 00	
Public School, do.	4 00	
Young Ladies at Ingham University, Leroy, N. Y.	13 25	
Miss Tracy's Seminary, Rochester, N. Y.	1 00	
Rev. Dr. Dewey, do.	1 00	
Academy at Wilson, N. Y.	2 80	
Baptist Church, do.	6 93	
Wm. P. Grout, do.	1 00	
Presbyt'n S. S., do.	4 39	
M. E. Church, do.	2 03	
Dr. Creswell, do.	1 00	
H. Hamlin, do.	25	
A. Goodenough, do.	25	
T. Pettit, do.	25	

Rev. N. Snell, for Universalist Lockport, N. Y.		5 00
Received at Exhibition, Drummondville, C. W.		2 00
Rev. E. S. Wright, Fredonia,		1 00
Wm. S. Lake,	do	50
Rev. S. A. Skinner, Westfield, N. Y.		1 00
D. A. Knowlton,	do.	5 00
S. A. Hungerford,	do.	1 00
Contributions at Prayer Meeting,		2 00
Henry Viets, Oberlin, Ohio,		4 00
Eagle St. School, Cleveland, Ohio.		4 00
1st Baptist S. S.	do.	6 41
1st Pres. Church,	do.	1 60
Plymouth S. S.,	do.	12 50
2d Pres. Church S. S.,	do.	7 18
St. Clair M. E. S. S.,	do.	4 00
Pupils of Rockwell St. Public School,	do.	4 00
3d Presbyterian S. S.,	do.	10 00
Cleveland Ladies' Seminary,	do.	2 80
Dr. Sealy's Water Cure,	do.	3 00
Dr. Sealy,	do.	1 00
2d Baptist S. S.	do.	4 45
Congregational Ch.,	do.	9 00
E. Ingersol, Dover Centre,		1 00
Mrs. R. P. Penfield, New York,		2 00
M. E. Church, Albion, N. Y.,		10 62
Baptist Church,	do.	6 38
Mrs. L. Burrows,	do.	1 50
Mr. R. S. Burrows,	do.	1 00
Contribution of Schools, by S. A. Brown,	do.	22
Seminary, Lima, N. Y.,		11 00
St. John M. E. Church, Rochester, N. Y.,		4 40
Universalist Church,	do.	9 00
Colored School, Lockport, N. Y.		33
J. H. Dewey, Manchester, N. Y.		1 00

M. E. S. S., Canandaigua, N. Y.	2	50
Mrs. Gregg,	do.	12 50
Mrs. Chapin,	do.	2 00
Rev. Mr. Dagget,	do.	50
Academy,	do.	4 50
Seminary,	do.	75
1st Baptist Church, do.		5 00
Dr. Cooke, Lunatic Asylum, do.	1	50
M. E. Church, Naples, N. Y.		5 00
M. E. Church, North Cohocton, N. Y.		2 80
Rev. A. S. Baker, Corning, N.Y.	1	00
Wm. Cunningham,	do.	1 00
E. S. Williams,	do.	1 00
Mrs. Bailey,	do.	1 00
A. N. Rogers,	do.	1 00
Mrs. Phelps,	do.	1 00
Kimble & Jewell,	do.	1 00
N. Robinson,	do.	1 00
S. F. Denton,	do.	1 00
R. Arnold,	do.	1 00
J. M. Wood,	do.	1 00
S. C. Robertson,	do.	1 00
N. C. Launey,	do.	1 00
N. R. Seeley,	do.	1 00
J. M. Smith,	do.	1 00
M. Hotchkiss,	do.	1 00
D. Chichester,	do.	1 00
L. H. Shattick,	do.	1 00
A. Olcott,	do.	1 00
Q. W. Wellington,	do.	1 00
C. D. Luce,	do.	50
Mrs. Pudney,	do.	1 50
Mr. Lucas,	do.	1 00
C. Page,	do.	1 00
A. C. Stearns,	do.	1 00
A. Jones,	do	1 00
R. E. Robinson,	do.	2 00
C. H. Soule,	do.	1 00
J. Hawes,	do.	1 00
F. Alcott,	do.	1 00
E. B. Smith,	do.	1 00
E. A. Jeffery,	do.	1 00
Mr. Corcoran,	do.	50

J. H. Conner,	Corning.	50	J. R. Balcon, Binghamton, N.Y.		1	00
B. Paine,	d o	50	Mrs. M. Whiting,	do.	1	00
Mr. Stevens,	do.	50	C. B. Campbell,	do.	1	00
O. G. Paine,	do.	50	Mrs. H. Mathers,	do.	3	00
Mr. Howard,	do.	50	J. E. New,	do.	1	00
Unknown,	do.	25	M. R. Mathers,	do.	3	00
"	do.	37	Mrs. Dickinson,	do.	1	50
G. W. Preston,	do.	50	Rev. Mr. Lockwood,	do.	1	00
Fletcher,	do.	50	Received by Dr. West, for			
E. Clisden,	do.	50	Young Ladies' Seminary,			
Miss M. Mortimer, Elmira, N.Y.		1 00	Buffalo, N. Y. _____		7	00
Mrs. E. Webster,	do.	50	A. B. Lawrence, Niagara			
Colored Church,	do.	4 73	Falls, N. Y. _____		5	00
1st M. E. S. S.,	do.	3 62	Presbyterian S. S. do.		10	00
Miss Thurston's Seminary, do.		2 00	Congregational Church, T.			
Miss Thurston,	do.	2 00	W. Fox, Pastor, Leroy, N. Y.		1	50
B. G. Carpenter,	do.	1 00	Episcopalian Church, R. T.			
S. W. Benjamin,	do.	1 00	Parvin, pastor, do.		6	72
Contribution at Dr. Gleason's			Presbyterian S. S. do.		13	00
Water Cure,	do.	5 36	I. G. Morgan, Plattsburg, N. Y.		1	00
Elmira College,	do.	10 46	Judge R. H. Boucher, Peter-			
J. W. Jamoreux, Owego, N. Y.		1 00	borough, C. W. _____		1	00
Presbyterian S. S.,	do.	10 00	Rec'd per children's boxes, &c.		37	00
Congregational S. S.,	do.	4 65	Cash borrowed, _____		5	00
E. Hawley, Binghamton, N. Y.		5 00	Amount received for provis-			
F. B. Fairchilds,	do.	1 00	ions sold, _____		46	06

Amount of cash receipts from Jan. 1st to July 1st, 1858,__$577 67

PROVISIONS, &c.

Rev. J. O. Knapp, Niagara City, N. Y., 5 chairs, 1 lounge.

J. L. Bennet, Lockport, N. Y., 1 bag of apples, &c.

Mr. Childs, Niagara City, N. Y., 1 bu. potatoes, 1 bu. turnips, cabbages, 1 comfortable, straw for beds, 1 load wood, use of team, &c.

James Watson, donation on stove, $11.

Mrs. Graves, Niagara City, N. Y., 1 bundle clothing, 1 comfortable.

Mrs. Adams, Niagara City, N. Y., 1 comfortable.

Mrs. Shepherd, Buffalo, N. Y. 1 quilt.

Mrs. C. Gildersleeve, Buffalo, N. Y., 2 pillows, 2 pillow-cases.

Clothing for children from the Barrack Mission School, Hamilton, C. W.

Mrs. Lathrop, Buffalo, N. Y., 1 quilt, 2 sheets.

Mrs. Dean, Niagara City, clothing for children.

J. Bias, Drummondville, C. W., 1 chicken, 1 bag potatoes, ½ bag apples, 1 doz. eggs, dried apples, peaches, &c.

A. Porter, Niagara Falls, N. Y., 1 load wood.

Mrs. A. Porter, Niagara Falls, N. Y. clothing for children.

D. Talbot, London, C. W., 1 pair shoes for blind girl.

J. M. Jones, parcel clothing for children.

Mrs. Barret, Albion, N. Y. 2 towels.

Young ladies of Ingham University, Leroy, N. Y., 1 box of clothing

Wm. Bird, Lockport, N. Y., 1 bbl. rye flour.

Dr. McChestney, Wilson, N. Y., ½ bu. beans, 1½ doz. eggs, 1 pk. apples, 1 bu. potatoes, 3 lbs pork.

Timothy Darling, Wilson, N. Y., 2 bu. buckwheat, 3 lbs butter.

J. M. Newman, Wilson, N. Y., 2 doz. eggs, 2 chickens, pork.

Widow Lockwood, Wilson, N. Y., 1 bu. buckwheat.

Mr. Stacey, Wilson, N.Y. 2 bu. buckwheat, 2 bu. barley, and butter.

Dea. Croxman, Wilson, N. Y., 1 bu. ears corn, ½ bu. buckwheat, 1 bu. peas, 1 cap, clothing for children.

Dea. Case, Wilson, N. Y., 1½ bu. potatoes.

Dea. Gales, Wilson, N. Y., 2 bu. beets, 2 doz. eggs, 1 quilt.

Mr. Hayne, Wilson, N. Y., 1 bu. potatoes.

Mr. Peere, Wilson, N. Y., ½ bu. beans.

Mr. Lockwood, Wilson, N. Y., 2 bu. buckwheat, 2 bu. barley, 2 bu. butter.

A. Dailey, Wilson, N. Y., 1 ham, ¾ bu. potatoes, ¾ bu. apples.

C. D. Ward, Wilson, N. Y., 2 bu potatoes.

Holmes & Brown, Wilson, N. Y. 2½ bu. potatoes, ½ bu. turnips, 17 lbs. pork.

Samuel Cutterback, 4 head cabbages, 1 bu. turnips, 1 bu. rye. 15 eggs.

A. Croxman, Wilson, N. Y., 1 bu. apples, 10 heads cabbage.

M. Pettit, Wilson, N. Y., 10 lbs. pork, butter.

I. Gifford, Wilson, N. Y. 1 bag of apples.

D. S. Armstrong, Wilson, N. Y., 2 bu. potatoes.

Mr Ellis, Wilson, N. Y., ½ bu. potatoes, ½ bu. turnips, onions, 5½ lbs. feathers, 3 coats, ½ bu. ears corn, 2 chickens.

D. V. W. Dox, Wilson, N. Y., 1 coat, 1½ bu. potatoes.

N. Davis, Wilson, N. Y. 1 bu. wheat.

Vincent Seeley, Wilson, N Y. cheese, 10 lbs. honey, 1 bu. parsnips.

I. Tower, Wilson, N. Y., use of team one day.

J. A. Knowles, Wilson, N. Y. 3 doz. eggs.

Wm. Knowles, Wilson, N. Y. 2 chickens, 6 lbs. soap, ½ bu. turnips, 2 towels, 1½ bu. apples.

Almira, Wilson, N. Y., 1 towel, dried apples.

J. E. Tower, Wilson, N. Y., 2½ bu. ears corn, 5 lbs. pork, 1½ bu. potatoes.

Royal Ide, Wilson, N. Y. 1 shoulder, 12 lbs. pork.

Elder Daniel Ide, Wilson, N., Y. 2 bu. potatoes, 1 quilt, 1 pair pillow cases.

F. Bawker, Wilson, N. Y., 1 hen.

I. Eggleston, Wilson, N. Y., 10 lbs. dried apples.

I. T. Woodberry, Wilson, N. Y., 12 lbs. beef.

N. Outwater, Wilson, N. Y., 5 bu. potatoes, 3 doz. eggs.

H. Hamlin, Wilson, N. Y., chickens, 9 lbs. pork.

Geo. Parker, Wilson, N. Y. 3 chickens, 1 chop.

M. E. Farr, Wilson, N. Y., 1 bu. wheat.

H. King, Wilson, N. Y., 1 bu. potatoes, 1 bu. turnips.

I. Burton, Wilson, N. Y., 5 lbs. beef, 5 lbs. pork, 1 pk. meal.

D. Timothy, Wilson, N. Y., 1 chop.

H. Maham, Wilson, N. Y., 1 bu. potatoes.

W. C. Webster, Wilson, N. Y., ½ bu. beans, 1 quilt, 1 pair pillow cases.

Daniel Folger, Wilson, N. Y. 2 bu. buckwheat, dried apples, pork.

Dea. O. Ferris, Wilson, N. Y., 2 bu. oats, 6 lbs. beef, 3 hens.

C. Edwards, Wilson, N. Y., 1 bed tick, 1 pair pillow cases, 1 sheet, pork.

C. Ward, Wilson, N. Y. 2 bu. potatoes.

I. Haynes, Wilson, N. Y., ½ bu. potatoes.

H. Pettit, Wilson, N. Y., 1 barrel apples.

O. Cole, Wilson, N. Y., 1 ham.

I. Billings, Wilson, N. Y., 1 bu. beans, 1 barrel apples.

A. McChestney, Wilson, N. Y. 1½ bu. potatoes.

Mrs. A. Pettit, Wilson, N. Y., 1 dress.

A. Pettit, Wilson, N. Y., 2 bu. potatoes, 2 chickens.

J. Johnson, Wilson, N. Y., 1 bu. buckwheat, 4 chops.

H. Johnson, Wilson, N. Y., 2 bu. wheat, 1 shoulder.

Dr. Taber, Wilson, N. Y., 1 bu. rye.

S. Sheldon, Wilson, N. Y., 2 bu. buckwheat.

C. Pettit, Wilson, N. Y., 1 bu. wheat.

S. Burch, Wilson, N. Y., 1 shoulder,

R. Rollinson, Wilson, N. Y., 1½ bu. turnips, ½ bu. beans, 7 lbs. pork.

S. Miller, Wilson, N. Y., 1 sheet, 2 pair pillow cases, 3 hens.

J. Swick, Wilson, N. Y., 1 bu. rye, 7 lbs. pork, 1 doz. eggs, 1 quilt, 1 pair pillow cases.

H. Lockwood, Wilson, N. Y., 2 chops.

H. Hotchkiss, Wilson, N. Y., 4 lbs. pork.

E. Brewer, Wilson, N. Y., 1 chicken.

R. Wilson, Wilson, N. Y., 2½ bu. apples, 32 lbs. pork.

C. Pettit, Wilson, N. Y., ½ bu. beans, 1 quilt.

S. Pettit, Wilson, N. Y. 7 lbs. pork, 1 chicken.

G. W. Loomis, Wilson, N. Y., 2 bu. potatoes, 1 bu. carrots, ½ bu. beets, 25 lbs. pork, ½ bu. apples, 2 doz. eggs, 1 sheet.

J. Pettit, Wilson, N. Y. 1½ bu. potatoes.

J. Wright, Wilson, N. Y., 2 chickens.

N. C. Ward, Wilson, N. Y., ½ bu. meal, 1 bu. potatoes, beef.

F. Loomis, Wilson, N. Y., 2 lbs. butter, 1 bu. corn.

N. Galup, Wilson, N. Y., 1 shoulder, beef.

A. Taber, Wilson, N. Y., 3 lbs. butter, 2 doz. eggs, 2 lbs. pork.

S. Taber, Wilson, N. Y., 1 chicken.

Mrs. Hotchkiss, Wilson, N. Y., 2 pillow cases.

H. S. Berry, Wilson, N. Y., 3 doz. eggs, ½ bu. corn, 6 lbs. pork, 1 bu. potatoes, 2 hens.

Mrs. Rockwood, Wilson, N.Y., 1 quilt.

G. W. Brickford, Wilson, N. Y., 1 bu. potatoes, 1 bu. corn, 1 straw tick, 11 hens.

Dea. Chapin, Wilson, N. Y., 1 bu. wheat, ½ bu. beans, 1 chop, 1 shoulder.

R. Rollinson, Wilson, N. Y., 1 bu. beans, 1 bu. parsnips, 4 lbs. pork.

Mr. Arnold, Wilson, N. Y., 2 chickens, 1 pk. pop corn, clothing, use of team 1 day.

A. Mix, Wilson, N. Y., 1 bu. rye, 3 bu. potatoes.

J. Samson, Wilson, N. Y., 4 smoked chops.

J. Moore, Wilson, N. Y., 1 ham.

S. Knowles, Wilson, N. Y., 2 pillow cases.

D. Brewer, Wilson, N. Y., 1 bu. beans, 1 bu. potatoes.

D. Carter, Wilson, N. Y., 1 ham.

Miller, Wilson, N. Y., ½ bu. wheat.

Dea. Holmes, Wilson, N. Y., 6 bu. potatoes, 1 ham, 1 chicken, clothing for boys, use of team 2 days.

C. Loomis, Wilson, N. Y., 1 box butter.

Mr. Dunlap, Elmira, N. Y., Book of Psalms in raised letters.

We desire also to thank the proprietors of the following valuable journals gratuitously furnished to the school:

Advocate and Family Guardian, New York City.

The Home, Buffalo, N. Y.

Canada Christian Advocate, Hamilton, C. W.

Lockport Daily Advertiser and Democrat.

Lockport Daily Courier.

Niagara Falls Gazette.

The Northern Independent, Auburn, N. Y.

EXPENDITURES.

Groceries and Provisions,	$63	79
Fares, ...	120	89
Fuel and lights, . .	25	00
Furniture, . . .	65	70
Freight and Cartage, .	32	69
Travelling expenses, .	90	43
Wages, . . .	18	58
Books and stationery, .	9	63
Hardware and crockery,	37	61
Repairs, ...	9	00
Postage and P. O. box,	7	66
Feed for cow, . . .	2	00
Clothing, . . .	8	68
Rent, ...	38	50
Articles at drug store,	2	12
Cow, ...	30	00
Seeds and plants for garden,	2	31
Printing and engraving, .	17	50
Paid Mrs. Skinner on salary,	38	50
	$620	59

Bills due on first of July,   . . . $41 13
Furniture, &c., on hand, ...   152 94

In reference to the donations from Wilson, we wish to say that it was with great difficulty that we have been able to give any correct account; those donations having been collected by several individuals; besides which the lists were more or less incorrect on account of having been written with a pencil, it was sometimes almost if not quite impossible to decipher them. But we have done the best we could under the circumstances, and we hope if mistakes are found that no one will charge us with wrong, but will send us the corrections which we will cheerfully publish in our next report.

This report was prepared and intended to have been published on the first of August, but it has been delayed for want of means to defray the expenses of publication. It has required all we could get to meet the current expenses of the school.

All communications should be sent to

P. H. SKINNER,

School for Colored Deaf, Dumb and Blind,
Niagara City, N. Y.

Bibliography

The Evolution of an Ethnic Neighborhood that Became United in Diversity: The East Side, Niagara Falls, New York 1880-1930. H. William Feder, Ph.D. From a paper in the Niagara Falls Memorial Library history records.

Dr. P.H. Skinner: Controversial Educator of the Deaf, Blind and Mute and Niagara Falls, New York, Abolitionist. Michael Boston, Ph.D., "Afro-Americans in New York Life and History." July 2005, pages 45-72.

Before They Could Vote, American Women's Autobiographical Writing, 1819-1919, edited by Sidonie Smith and Julia Watson. "A Brief Narrative of the Life of Mrs. Adele M. Jewel."

The Mute and the Blind (published 1859 through the mid-1860s), a newspaper published by Dr. Skinner. Copies of some issues are available for research through the Niagara County Historian (139 Niagara Street, Lockport, NY 14094), Houghton Library at Harvard University (Harvard Yard, Cambridge, MA 02138), Old Sturbridge Village (1 Old Sturbridge Village Road, Sturbridge, MA 01566), Gallaudet University Archives (800 Florida Avenue N.E., Washington, DC 20002), and the Museum of disABILITY History (3826 Main Street, Buffalo, NY 14226, 716.629.3626).